Murder in Montauk

MICHIGAN
Reading Plus
READERS

Murder in Montauk

Judy Soloway Kay

THE UNIVERSITY OF MICHIGAN PRESS

Ann Arbor

To my husband, Chet

*Thank you for your encouragement, advice,
and especially, your love.*

Contents

Montauk, Long Island

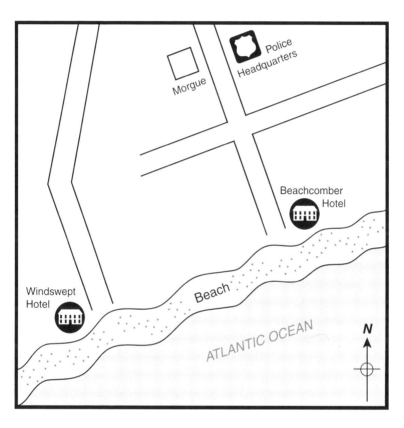

Detailed map of Montauk

Characters

CHARLIE ANDERSON
A sportswriter for the *Boston Globe*
BETH ANDERSON
Charlie Anderson's wife of nearly six years
BARRY MILTON
Charlie Anderson's editor at the *Boston Globe*
POLICE CHIEF MALKIN
Police Chief of Montauk, Long Island
DEPUTY O'ROURKE
A rookie officer on the Montauk police force
DAVID GILDEN
A man found dead in a hotel in Montauk,
Long Island
MR. PARKER
The manager of the Beachcomber Hotel

Chapter 1

Who Am I?

WHEN CHARLIE ANDERSON was ten years old, he found out he was adopted. He could never forget that night. It was right after dinner. Charlie was watching television. Mom and Dad both came into the living room. Dad turned off the TV and said in a serious voice, "Charlie, there's something your mother and I want to talk to you about."

Mom looked very serious, too, and Charlie started to worry that something was very wrong. "What's the matter, Dad?" he asked.

"Well, son, your Mom and I have waited to talk to you about this until you were the right age, and now that you're ten, we think you can understand what we're going to tell you."

"What's going on? Is someone sick or dead?" Charlie asked.

"No, dear, it's nothing like that. We just want you to know that when you were born, we weren't your birth parents," Mom started to explain.

"What? What do you mean? You're my parents."

"Of course, we're your parents, but what I mean is, we adopted you."

ADOPTED. ADOPTED. The word rang in Charlie's ears and thoughts. It was as if someone had hit him.

He knew he should have asked questions, but instead he just wanted to run away from his parents and not think about the information he had just been given.

He said, "You're wrong. I don't believe you. You're just playing around." When his Dad came to put his arm around him, Charlie pushed him away and ran to his room. He heard his mother crying as he ran up the steps.

The next morning at breakfast, Charlie asked some questions, and his parents tried to answer them. "Who are my birth parents? Where was I born? Why didn't they want me? Do they know where I am now?"

Charlie found out that his birth parents had lived in another part of Wisconsin and were very poor. They didn't have the money to raise another child, and so they put him up for adoption. An agency had advertised in the newspaper, and Mr. and Mrs. Anderson answered the ad. As it turned out, Charlie was one of a set of twins; his brother had died at birth.

"You mean I had a twin brother?" Charlie asked.

"Yes, Charlie, but he was sick and didn't make it," Mom told him. Charlie seemed more interested in this part of his birth story than anything else.

Dad continued, "We never met your parents, but we loved you from the first minute we saw you. You were in a blue blanket. Your thumb was in your mouth, and your curls were peeking out from under a little blue hat."

Charlie said, "Now I understand about my hair. Everyone always said I don't look anything like either one of you. You both have straight, blond hair, and I've got dark, curly hair."

The first few weeks it was hard for Charlie to stop thinking about being adopted, but after awhile, he was busy with school activities. As a fourth grader he was trying out for the town's all-star baseball team, and everyone said he had a good chance of making it. One day he ran in the door after school and shouted, "I made it! I made it! I'm on the team!"

Dad was traveling for business, but Mom was home. They went out for dinner, and he ordered a big piece of chocolate cake for dessert. When they arrived home, they called Dad at the hotel to tell him the good news. Dad was very pleased.

"I'm so happy for you, son."

"It's because you practiced with me all summer, pitching to me and playing catch. I never could have done it without you, Dad."

Dad was quiet for awhile. Charlie couldn't see that, on the other end of the phone, his father was wiping his eyes with a handkerchief.

"Are you there, Dad?"

"I'm here. I can't wait to go to your games, Charlie."

Chapter 2

Everything He Wanted

THE YEARS WENT BY, and Charlie's love for baseball continued. He played on his high school team and was an excellent student. He was very interested in writing and won a scholarship from Yale University. Four years later when he graduated from Yale, he started working at a newspaper in New York City. He covered all kinds of news stories. Not long after that, he was offered a job at the *Boston Globe.* In a short while, he was writing sports articles. His love for baseball showed in his writing, and he became well known across the country as a sportswriter.

While he was at Yale, Charlie met Beth, a law student. They started dating and got married a few years after they finished school. Charlie now had everything he wanted—a wife, a great job, and the chance to travel. He was thirty years old, six feet tall, and thin. He still had dark, curly hair, but he was starting to see a few gray hairs.

Charlie and Beth had never talked about having children. Because they were married when they were young, babies were not part of their immediate plans. They were enjoying a period of time just working hard at their jobs. Then one day Beth said to Charlie, "When are we going to have a baby?"

Charlie was quiet.

"Did you hear me, Charlie?"

"Yes, I heard you. I don't know, Beth. What makes you bring it up now?"

"Well, we've been married for over five years, and I want to have a child. Don't you?"

"I don't know. I haven't really thought about it. I like it being just the two of us. Babies change things. I don't want to change things."

"Well, let's think about it, Charlie. Okay? Let's just think about it."

"Beth, there's something you should know. I never told you that I was adopted. My parents are great, but they aren't my biological parents. I don't know much about my background. How can we have a baby when I don't know my history? What if there is some genetic problem we don't know about?"

"Charlie, why didn't you tell me? I understand the reason that you're worried, but we can go for genetic analysis to learn if there is any evidence of a problem." She smiled at him and said, "See, you don't need to worry."

But Charlie did worry. Every time Beth talked about going to the doctor for the tests, Charlie found some reason not to go. He was either traveling or too busy at work. After awhile, she stopped asking. Beth and Charlie began to go their separate ways. Each worked a lot, and Beth no longer talked about having a baby. Right before their sixth wedding anniversary, Beth told Charlie she wanted them to separate.

"Charlie, I just think it would be better for both of us if we spent some time away from each other. You're involved with your work, and you travel so much that I never see you. Our schedules always seem to conflict. I have a chance to become a partner in my law firm, and I'll be busy with meetings and travel. We've grown apart, and we're just kidding ourselves by staying together."

"Beth, what's happened to us? We were so close, and now we never really talk. We don't have fun anymore. I guess it's my fault for traveling so much, but even when I'm in town, you're always at the office. Our marriage doesn't seem to be as important to either of us anymore."

"I guess you're right, Charlie. I never thought we'd end up like this."

"Maybe after being on our own, we'll get back together again. I'll move out. You stay here in the house. I'm the one who's always traveling anyway."

"I'll leave that decision up to you, Charlie. You know where I'll be."

Chapter 3

Taking Some Time Off

ONE DAY, Charlie went to see his editor, Barry Milton. "Barry," he said, "I've decided to take some time off over the summer. I hope that's okay with you. There's a book I've always wanted to write, and I'll need some free time. I'll call in to check on things here."

"Well, Charlie. This is a bit of a surprise, but then I'm used to surprises in this business. Is this book a secret?"

"Not really, but I'm not telling anyone about it," Charlie laughed.

"Okay, my friend, I'm sure you know what you're doing. If you need me, just call. What about Beth?"

"We haven't told anyone, but we've been having some problems and we're separating for awhile. It was a mutual decision."

"I'm sorry to hear that. I have always thought of you two as the perfect couple."

"I guess we're just like everyone else."

"Good luck, Charlie. Keep in touch."

"Thanks, Barry."

Charlie had some phone calls to make. He wanted to write a historical book about baseball, and now that he and Beth had parted, it seemed to be a good time to write it. He had always wanted to live in the Maine woods. As soon as this idea came to him, he knew it was right.

First, he called Beth. He told her he was going away on a trip, so she wouldn't worry. Then he called a real estate agent and began to look for a house. His four-wheel drive Jeep would come in handy in Maine.

The real estate agent Elizabeth Enright had the biggest ads in the newspaper, so Charlie called her. She had a few houses available to rent. The one he really liked was on a dirt road that led to a lake. There was a big fireplace, a canoe, and lots of bird houses. The couple that owned it was traveling through Europe, and would be away until October.

"They'll be happy to know they're renting it to a writer," said Ms. Enright. "If you want it, I'll have the necessary papers ready in forty-eight hours."

Charlie drove up from Boston and moved in on July 1. The first night in the house he was surprised by the sound of the loons that lived on the lake. He remembered reading a book about loons and learning that they mate for life. "They stay together longer than many people," he thought sadly.

He was glad he packed his sweaters and socks. Even in July, the night air was cooler than in the city.

The next morning he woke up to the sound of

birds singing, and he took a deep breath when he opened the door. The air was clean and clear. There was a strong smell of pine from the pine trees that grew near the house.

Charlie stretched his arms out wide and said, "It's good to be alive." For the first time in a long time, he was happy. Even though there had been many changes in his life, he felt at peace with himself.

"I know I made the right decision to come here. The environment feels right for writing." Then Charlie laughed, "I've been talking to myself. I'll probably be doing that a lot now that I'm up here in the Maine woods alone."

He had decided not to bring a TV, and the one in the house was broken. "That's just as well. I don't want any world news interrupting my work. I like being isolated out here."

He had his computer and his cell phone for emergencies. No one knew where he was. His friends thought he was traveling. He told Beth he would call once a week just to see how she was. She knew he wanted to be alone. They had parted in a friendly way, and each one cared about how the other was doing.

Charlie suddenly realized that he hadn't eaten since the night before. "I'd better go into town and get some food, or I won't be doing any work. I could really go for a cup of coffee." He sat down at the kitchen table and wrote out a shopping list. He included lots of canned goods. Food had never been very important to Charlie, and he wasn't much of a cook. "I'm going to have to learn to cook if I want to live out here," he thought.

§🐦

The town of Camden was small and quiet. There was a market called Best Market, which seemed funny to Charlie since it was the only one in town. He filled his shopping basket with coffee, tuna fish, canned vegetables, frozen fish sticks, ground beef, several loaves of bread, peanut butter and jelly, and some snack foods. The last thing he added was chocolate ice cream. It was his favorite.

After getting home and putting the food away, Charlie took the canoe out on the lake. It was a lovely afternoon. The sun was strong, but a breeze made it very comfortable. Charlie forgot the time. He paddled around the whole lake, and looked at all the other houses. By the time he got back, it was almost five o'clock. "I can't keep spending days like this, or I won't write more than a title for my book," he thought. "But I enjoyed the day, and tomorrow I'll get down to work."

He had already created a plan for writing his book. He would wake up each morning and go for a walk in the woods. After breakfast, he would work for a few hours. Then he would take a break for lunch and write some more in the afternoon. Before dinner, he would do some reading and editing. If he was tired of working, he would go for a ride in the car or go out in the canoe. Charlie knew he needed a routine if he was going to get a lot of writing done. He anticipated a busy yet relaxing summer. All in all, he felt pleased with his plan. Little did he know that the future would change everything.

Chapter 4

A Strange Discovery

ON JULY 8, a week after he had settled into his new home, Charlie was working on the computer. When he checked the news online, he found a news story about a man's body that had been discovered in a seaside hotel in Montauk, Long Island. When Charlie looked at the photograph of the man's face, his eyes opened wide. It was as if he were looking in the mirror. "Oh, my God, he looks just like me!"

Charlie read the news story and then printed it out.

MONTAUK, N.Y.—A man was found dead in a hotel on Montauk, Long Island, early Saturday morning by the owner of the hotel who had come by to check the room. There was no identification on the man, but he is thought to be Charles Anderson, a sportswriter for the *Boston Globe.* Anderson was on leave from the *Boston Globe* to work on a book, said his editor, Barry Milton. Milton said he didn't know where Anderson had gone, but Anderson said he would call Milton from time to time to "check in." Milton hadn't heard from him since June when he left Boston. Anderson is originally from Wisconsin. His wife, from whom he was separated, is flying from Boston to New York to identify the body. Police are looking for leads in the case and have posted a special telephone number for information: 800-555-7000.

Charlie read the story again and stared at the photo. He knew it wasn't him. He was sitting in a chair in front of his computer in the woods in Maine. "What in the world is going on? Why is my photo in this story about a dead man?" He was just about to call Beth when the thought came to him: "It isn't me, but who is it? He looks like my clone or my twin."

The word *twin* brought up an old memory. He remembered that his parents had told him many years ago, when he learned that he was adopted, that he was a twin. What if they were wrong and his twin hadn't died? What if the man they found was his identical twin? If so, how did he die? Was he killed? Charlie didn't know what to do. Initially, he wanted to tell people that he was alive and well, but he also wanted to find out who killed a man who looked just like him.

"I've got to find out if my twin brother did live. Let's see how good a researcher I am."

Charlie went online and checked hospital records all over Wisconsin for births on his birthdate. He was able to narrow the search to twin births, which made the job much easier. Finally, he found a hospital in

Bradley, a small town in northern Wisconsin, with a record of twin boys having been born to a Mary Gilden. The date matched. His next step was to call the hospital to see if there was any record of the death of one of the twins. A helpful young woman in the Records Department told him that both twins were sent home four days after birth. She told him to check the town and school records for more information. She even gave him the phone numbers. As he was about to thank her, she asked, "Do you want to know their names?"

"Sure. Do you have them?"

"They were Daniel and David."

After he hung up the phone, Charlie thought, "I wonder which one I was, Daniel or David? I'll find out my twin brother's name when I check other records. Then I'll know my original name."

A clerk in the Town Hall was also very helpful. He said that a David Gilden had been in kindergarten at Sims Elementary School and had graduated from Central High School.

"That means my original name was Daniel Gilden. I wonder what my life would have been like if I had grown up with my twin brother, David."

Charlie spent the rest of the day on the computer putting his journalistic skills to use. He checked military records, credit card companies, marriage licenses, and the Department of Motor Vehicles. He felt as if he was getting a picture of his twin brother, and he was surprised at how similar their lives were. "He got married the same year that I married Beth. I wonder if they have separated, too. He obtained his driver's license in the same year I did, and he owned a red Mustang. My first car was a red Mustang."

Charlie's brother, David, had served in the Army Reserves and worked in Special Operations overseas during the Gulf War. Charlie knew that meant he did intelligence work. "That could explain his sudden death. Maybe he was killed because he knew things that others wanted kept secret."

Charlie got most of his information from copies of old newspapers that he was able to access on the Internet. The small town of Bradley kept close tabs on David. When he had entered the service, there was a picture of him in uniform on the front page. Charlie felt sad seeing the photo. "I never knew you, Brother," he thought, "but I'm going to find out what happened to you in Montauk. It's the least I can do."

Charlie knew he would have to travel to Montauk to find out more about his brother. Obviously, he'd have to look different. He decided to dye his hair gray to make himself look older. He hadn't shaved since he arrived in Maine, so his beard had been growing for a week. He was surprised at how gray his beard was. It made him look older. Dark-rimmed glasses also helped disguise him. Maybe people would believe that he was an older cousin of Charlie's.

It had grown dark outside, and Charlie realized that his book would have to wait. He decided to fly to

New York. Then he thought, "No, I can't do that because I will have to show my ID. I'll have to drive to Montauk in the morning. I know it's at least a two-day trip."

He realized he hadn't eaten lunch. He'd been on the computer for hours! He ate a peanut butter and jelly sandwich for dinner and fell asleep wondering about his brother's life.

Chapter 5

Montauk

CHARLIE LEFT EARLY the next morning. His plan was to drive as much as he could and stop overnight somewhere outside of New York City. He made a short stop near Boston to fill up with gasoline and picked up a copy of the *Boston Globe*. His photograph was on the front page. He read his obituary and thought, "Well, it's nice to know I'll be missed." He finally felt his eyes closing and decided to stop for the night at a motel. He planned to start out for Montauk early the next morning to try to beat the rush-hour traffic. He guessed it was about a four-hour drive to the end of Long Island. He had been in Montauk once before about five years ago for a story. He remembered that some boys from Montauk had drowned. (This was when he wrote about general news events and before he became a sportswriter.) He remembered the police chief, a big, six-foot-four muscular fellow and a former Marine. Malkin. That was his name. He wondered if Chief Malkin was still head of the police force. Maybe he could help Charlie.

Charlie's main concern was what to do when he saw Beth. The news article said she was coming to Montauk to identify the body. The more he thought about it, the more Charlie realized he needed her help.

"If I confide in Beth and tell her about my twin brother, she can assist me. She can go places and ask questions that I can't. Who am I kidding? I really want to talk to her. I miss her. It's only been a few weeks since we separated, but I miss her. I wonder if she misses me. I wonder if she's sad that I'm dead. This is crazy!"

His thoughts and the radio helped pass the time, and soon Charlie saw the sign for Montauk Point. It was noon, and Charlie decided to stop for lunch at a roadside diner called The Lunch Break. He remembered it from his last trip. They served the best lobster rolls.

"It's ironic. I just came from a week in Maine, and I didn't have lobster once. Now, I'm here in Montauk. I had to drive two days for a lobster roll." He pulled over and went in.

Chapter 6

I Wonder Why
He Was Here

WHEN CHARLIE ENTERED THE RESTAURANT, he noticed that Police Chief Malkin was sitting at a table with one of his deputies. Charlie could see Malkin from a distance, but he couldn't see Charlie. He thought that Chief Malkin may be helpful later. When the waitress came over to his table, Charlie ordered a lobster roll and a lemonade. It was starting to get hot, and a cold lemonade sounded good.

After lunch Charlie checked into the Windswept Hotel on the beach. Fortunately, he was able to make a reservation from Maine. This was the busy season, but he was able to reserve a room because of a last-minute cancellation.

After he unpacked, Charlie took a walk near the ocean. It was a beautiful stretch of beach, and all he saw for miles were sand, sky, and water. The day was clear, and there were some people swimming, but it wasn't crowded. He could see a few brightly colored umbrellas and towels, but the natural beauty of the beach was unspoiled. It was hard to believe that his brother was murdered here. Yes, the more Charlie thought about it, the more he got the feeling that his brother was murdered. He was found in a hotel a half mile east on the beach.

"I wonder why he was here? Was he on an assignment? I can't believe he committed suicide. The newspapers made it sound as if he had killed himself, but from what I know about him, I don't buy that. I have a reporter's hunch that there was foul play. Maybe I've been reading too many crime novels, but my journalist's sixth sense says it was murder.

"I've got to talk to Malkin before Beth arrives. I'll pretend I'm a cousin. Hopefully, I look different enough now that he won't recognize me. I'll say I live in New York City and that I drove out to see what happened."

That afternoon Charlie went to police headquarters. Fortunately, the chief wasn't there. A rookie officer named Rick O'Rourke told Charlie what he knew about the case. He said that the death seemed to be a suicide.

Charlie asked, "Did he leave a note?"

O'Rourke answered, "Yeah, there was a typed note saying he was tired of living a lie."

"Did he sign the note?"

"No, there was no signature"

"Well, isn't that strange?"

"Yeah, I thought so, but the chief said that sometimes that happens."

"How did he kill himself?" Charlie asked.

"Pills and alcohol. It's a bad combination."

Charlie shook his head, which the rookie interpreted as sorrow. What Charlie was really thinking was that someone can hold a gun to your head and force you to take pills and alcohol. Either way you die. Whoever did this to David wanted to keep him silent. "I wonder what my brother was involved in," Charlie thought. "Drugs? Gambling? CIA? I've got to find out."

"Were you close cousins? I mean did you grow up near each other?" O'Rourke asked.

"No, my folks moved east, and we only saw each other at Christmas and family weddings."

"Yeah, that happens to a lot of families. I've lived in this town my whole life. My father and grandfather were both born here. They were fishermen, like everybody else here. I'm the first cop in the family. I like the water, but I get seasick."

"Well, thanks, Officer O'Rourke. I appreciate your talking to me."

"No problem. By the way, what did you say your name is, and where are you staying in case the chief wants to get in touch with you?"

Charlie answered, "Andy. Andrew Anderson." It was the first name that popped into his head. "I'm at the Windswept Hotel."

Officer O'Rourke wrote down the information as Charlie (Andy) left the office.

Chapter 7

A Bad Dream

CHARLIE COULDN'T SLEEP. He couldn't stop thinking about David. What was he like? How were they the same? Even though they had been brought up in different homes, they shared the same genetic history. Charlie did some research on twins and read case histories of twins who were brought up separately. In many cases, twins separated lead very similar lives. Even though he never met David, Charlie felt as if he knew him. If anyone could find out who killed David, it was Charlie.

When he finally fell asleep, Charlie had a dream about being in the ocean. It was a beautiful, sunny day. The ocean was calm, and he was floating on his back. Suddenly, the sky grew dark and the water became very rough. Charlie was fighting to swim to land. He kept swimming hard and breathing quickly, but the land seemed far away. He woke up sweating and out of breath. Charlie's heart was beating quickly. The dream seemed so real, and he thought about it over and over again the next day.

In the morning Charlie took a walk along the beach. As he was walking, he decided to call Beth and let her know he was alive. He knew Beth could keep a secret, and he wanted to share his ideas with her. Remembering his dream made him want to reach out to Beth. He dialed her cell phone number.

"Hello, Beth. It's me, Charlie. Don't be afraid. If there's anyone around you, just stay calm. Don't ask any questions. Just listen to me. The man who is dead isn't me. I'm alive, and I'm fine. For now, until I get to the bottom of things, I want people to believe that I *am* dead. I need to talk to you. Are you alone?"

"Yes, I'm alone," she answered. "I just arrived at MacArthur Airport in Islip. Where are you?"

"I can't tell you now. I have to meet you."

"What happened? Please talk to me. I can't believe this!"

"I know. I know. I can't believe it either."

"Are you all right? I mean, really all right."

"I'm fine, Beth. Can you meet me tonight?"

"Of course, I can. I have to rent a car and drive to Montauk. Where should I meet you?"

"Do you remember the hotel we stayed at in Southampton? It's called the Hampton Arms."

"I remember. It was such a special weekend, and we loved the restaurant there."

"Beth," he said, "don't be surprised if you don't recognize me at first. I look a little different."

"What do you mean?"

"You'll see. I'll make a reservation for 7:00 tonight."

"I'll be there. And Charlie, I'm so glad you're okay."

"Thanks. See you tonight."

Chapter 8

Meeting Andy

BETH WALKED INTO THE RESTAURANT at the Hampton Arms. It was still called Henry's, named for the owner's dog who had passed away. Photographs of Henry hung on the walls along with awards he had won in American Kennel Club shows.

"Some things never change," Beth thought, and she smiled.

When the host asked if he could seat her, Beth said that she was waiting for a friend.

"Is the name Anderson?"

"Yes. How do you know?"

"He described you very well. Right this way, Miss." He led Beth to a table on the terrace with a view of the water. Beth's eyes and mouth opened wide when she saw Charlie. She was so happy to see him after thinking that he was dead.

"Hi, Beth, it's good to see you," said Charlie, and he held her tightly in his arms.

"Hi," she whispered. "Is that really you, Charlie?"

"Yes. Sit down. We have a lot to talk about. You

must be tired after flying. Waiter, please bring me the wine list."

"Oh, my God, Charlie, I can't believe it's you. If not for your voice, I wouldn't know you."

"Beth, it's *so* good to see you. I've been dealing with this alone, and it's driving me crazy."

"Tell me what happened."

The waiter arrived with the wine list, and Charlie ordered a bottle.

"I found out about my death the same way you did," he said. "I read it in the newspaper online while I was in Maine."

"But who is the man who died?"

"He was my twin brother."

"You said your brother died right after he was born."

"That's what I was told, but, actually, he was alive."

"All these years?"

"Yes," said Charlie. "All these years."

"Did your parents know?" Beth asked.

"No, I don't think so. They were told he had died. My biological mother must have changed her mind about giving both of us up for adoption. She never told them my brother was alive."

"Charlie, why didn't you tell the police about your brother?"

"I think he was murdered."

"But the papers said it was a suicide."

"Don't believe everything you read in the papers," he said with a big smile.

"Spoken like a true journalist," she said. "Why do

you think he was murdered?"

"I don't know, Beth. Suicide just doesn't fit. From what I know about him, it just doesn't make sense. You can call it my journalist's instinct."

"Did he leave a suicide note?"

"That's just what I asked. He typed a note but didn't sign it. Doesn't that seem unusual?"

"Well, there could be a reason," she said. "Maybe I should meet with the police chief. Let me see what I can find out."

"You'll also probably be asked to identify the body."

"Oh, no! How am I going to get through that?"

"Do you want me to go with you?"

"Yes, but who will you say you are?"

"I'm Cousin Andy from New York."

"Andy Anderson. That's very original." She laughed.

"Yeah, I know. It was the first thing that popped into my mind when I was at Police Headquarters."

"I guess I'd better start calling you Andy."

"That's a good idea. Here comes the waiter with our wine. We'll continue after he leaves."

The waiter brought them their wine.

"Charlie, I mean Andy, when did you see the police?"

"I was there this afternoon."

"Did you speak to the chief?" she asked. "Remember when you were out here years ago to cover that story about the three teenagers who drowned?"

"No, he wasn't there. I spoke to the deputy."

"When we go to identify the body, don't do much talking. He might recognize your voice. Let me talk to him and see what I can find out. As your, I mean, as Charlie's wife, I'll want to find out what he knows about Charlie."

"That's a good idea."

"I'll say I want to make funeral arrangements. I'll ask to see the suicide note, and I'll wear dark glasses, so I can pretend to be crying."

"You sound like a natural detective, Beth." He took her hand. "It's so good to have you here."

"I missed you, and when I thought you were dead, I felt so empty."

"So, you're glad to see me?"

"Of course, I never wanted you to leave in the first place. I didn't want you to move out."

"But, I thought you did. I thought you would be glad I left."

"I told you to leave because I hoped you would say you wanted to stay and work on our marriage."

"Maybe we'll both get another chance when this is all over. Let's drink to us, Beth, and to the future."

"Here's to us and to solving this mystery."

Chapter 9

The Morgue

Beth and Charlie arrived at the morgue early the next morning. Beth had a headache, and she knew it was her nerves. Charlie didn't tell Beth that he was nervous, but his hands were sweating and his heart was beating very fast. The attendant showed them into a white tiled room. While they waited, neither one spoke. Soon the attendant wheeled in a cart covered by a white sheet. The outline of a body was evident. When the attendant lifted the sheet, Beth gasped and started to cry. The resemblance to Charlie was so strong that for a moment she thought it was Charlie's dead body in front of her.

When the attendant asked her, "Is this your husband?" she began to sob again. "Yes," she responded.

Charlie put his arm around her shoulders, and they walked out. There were papers Beth had to sign before they could leave. Outside the morgue, they walked to the car as quickly as possible.

Without saying a word, Charlie headed for the beach. They parked the car, took off their shoes, and walked into the ocean. The water felt clean and cold. Both of them breathed the cool air and smelled the water. After a while Beth broke the silence.

"That was horrible. I never want to do that again."

"You were great. I'm sorry you had to go through that."

"It wasn't just seeing a dead body. He looked just like you. I felt as if I were looking at you."

"I know. It was eerie for me, too."

"Well, Detective Anderson, where do we go from here?"

"Let's be logical. Who would want to kill David?"

"What kind of work did he do?"

"He worked for the government. Maybe he knew something, and the government agency wanted to get rid of him."

"Maybe he was an agent and he found out something about a foreign government, and they killed him. Was he married?"

"Yes."

"Maybe his wife killed him for his insurance."

"We're not getting anywhere. We're going around in circles with our ideas. Let's find out why he came here. That might give us a clue."

"Good idea. Why don't you talk to Chief Malkin and see what he knows."

"I'll head over there now."

"Let's just wait a little while longer. The beach is so peaceful now. I feel as if we have it all to ourselves. Let's walk along the shore for awhile."

"Charlie, I've never seen you like this. You've changed."

"I know. It isn't every day you see yourself dead. It makes you think about your life and what's important."

Chapter 10

The Meeting with Chief Malkin

BETH DROVE TO POLICE HEADQUARTERS and asked to see Chief Malkin. "What a big guy," she thought as he stood up to meet her when she walked into his office.

"Hello, Mrs. Anderson. I'm sorry about your husband."

"Thank you," Beth answered and sat down facing his desk.

"The coroner's office told me you identified the body."

"Yes, I did. Chief Malkin, I'd like to know what you know about my husband's death."

"All right, Ma'am. I'll tell you what I know. I got a call from the owner of the Beachcomber Hotel. He's the one who found your husband. We rushed over, my deputy and me. The owner hadn't touched anything, and I called the crime lab people who came right over. They found the suicide note."

"Did it look as if anyone else had been in the

room?" asked Beth. "I can't believe Charlie would have killed himself."

"No one likes to believe that about a loved one. Anyway, we found his note."

"Did he sign it?"

"No, but it was written on his computer."

"Well then, anyone could have written it."

"Mrs. Anderson, I know it's hard to accept the fact that your husband killed himself, but the evidence makes it obvious."

"Chief Malkin, I'd like to see the suicide note."

He looked in the file on his desk and handed her the note. She read it slowly.

"This doesn't sound like Charlie. It's not the way he writes. I've read his writing for years. This doesn't sound like him. Anyone could have typed it on his computer and printed it out."

"You think someone else wrote this and murdered him?"

"Isn't that a possibility?"

"But who would want to kill your husband?"

"I have no idea, but you're the detective. I would like you to explore that possibility."

"All right. I'll be in touch. Just leave your phone number with Deputy O'Rourke."

Chief Malkin rose as Beth prepared to leave. She didn't bother to say "thank you," and neither one said "goodbye."

After she'd gone, Malkin said to O'Rourke, "That's one determined woman. She doesn't think her husband killed himself. She thinks he was murdered." He laughed.

O'Rourke said, "But he left a suicide note."

"She thinks someone else wrote it."

"Maybe she's right, Chief," O'Rourke said.

"What are you talking about? You were with me when we went to the hotel. You saw him and the note."

"I didn't come with you. I met you there, remember?"

"Either way, you saw the note."

"Yeah, you're right, Chief. I'm just trying to keep an open mind. You said I should do that when I'm on a case."

"Well, this case is closed as far as I'm concerned."

O'Rourke asked, "What should I do about calling her? She left her number and told me to call."

"Wait a couple of days, and then tell her we have no leads. I've got other things to do. You know the election's coming up, and I've got speeches and campaigning to do."

"Okay, Chief. I'll deal with Mrs. Anderson. Leave it to me."

Later on Beth met Charlie. She was angry, and Charlie saw it by the look on her face.

"What's the matter, Beth?

"That police chief. I don't like his attitude. He makes me angry."

"What happened?"

"He never investigated anything. He never looked into the possibility of murder. I told him the note wasn't written by Charlie. I said it wasn't his style. He looked very uncomfortable when I said that. I wonder if he knows who killed David?"

"Maybe *he* killed David."

"But why?

"I don't know, but the fact that he's so willing to call it a suicide makes me suspicious."

Beth jumped up suddenly and said, "We have to get hold of David's computer. It may give us some information about why he came here and who may have killed him."

"That's a great idea. It must be at Police Head-quarters."

"I'll go back this afternoon and ask for his possessions."

"I'll go with you."

Chapter 11

The Password

CHARLIE AND BETH ENTERED the police station. Charlie said, "Hello, Deputy."

O'Rourke looked up from his computer. "Hello, there. Andy Anderson, isn't it?"

"You've got a good memory. This is Mrs. Anderson, Charlie's wife."

"Yes, I know. We met this morning."

"We've come to get Charlie's things," said Beth. "Do you have them?"

"Yes, we do. Sorry you had to come back for them. I could have given them to you this morning, but you left in a hurry. I'll go get them for you." He went in a back room and returned with a suitcase and a paper bag.

"Where's Charlie's computer?" asked Beth.

"Oh, the Chief has that."

Beth and Charlie look at each other. Beth asked, "Why does he have it?"

"I don't know, Ma'am."

"Well, I would like to take it now. As Charlie's wife, it belongs to me."

"Okay, ma'am, I'm sure the Chief won't mind. It's right on his desk."

O'Rourke went into Malkin's office and brought out a laptop computer.

"Where is the Chief?" asked Charlie.

"He's giving a speech at the local Women's Gardening Club. He's running for mayor, and the special election is in two months."

"May I please have the computer, Deputy O'Rourke? Let's go, Andy."

"Okay, Beth." Charlie whispered to O'Rourke, "She's having a hard time. We appreciate your help."

As he was walking out the door, Charlie turned to the deputy. "On the night you found my cousin's body, did you and the Chief drive out together, or did you meet him there?"

"I met him there. He was on his way back from a speech, and he was closer, so we just met at the hotel."

"So you received the call in the office?"

"Yeah, I got the call from the hotel owner. It's the first death I've had to deal with."

"Well, thanks again, Deputy."

"Take care. I'm real sorry about your cousin."

Charlie and Beth went back to Charlie's hotel.

"Now that we have the computer, how are we going to open his files?" asked Beth. "We need his password."

"Let me work on it."

"Okay. I'll go get us some sandwiches and coffee. What do you want?"

"Just surprise me."

Beth came back about twenty minutes later and handed Charlie a grilled ham and cheese sandwich and a cup of coffee. "They didn't have much at the place down the road, and I wanted to get back quickly."

"That's fine. I like ham and cheese."

Beth looked at the computer and saw that Charlie had opened David's files. "How did you find out the password?" she asked.

"I tried some words based on what I know about his life. People usually use old addresses or phone numbers. Then I tried some of my own passwords and, sure enough, MUSTANG worked. It was his first car.

"Look, Beth. I opened some of his files. He did work for the CIA, but that was a while ago. The last entry was last year. He was working on something that seems to be fiction, but I think a lot of it is auto-biographical. He writes about an agent doing under-cover work in Morocco. He takes care of another agent who's injured during a shooting. They're both hiding out in a building. I wonder if this really hap-pened to David. He writes very well and describes his characters as if they were real people. His writing shows his interest in foreign places, and he makes the story come alive."

"Charlie, do you think he discovered something

new, and whoever knew about it killed him to keep him quiet?"

"It could be. You know, Beth, it's interesting that he, too, discovered a need to write as I did."

Beth touched his arm and said, "Charlie, I'm so sorry you lost your brother."

"I never really had him, Beth, but I wish I had known him. It would have been fun growing up together and hanging out. Anyway, I don't see any files on anything he was working on in Montauk. We've gone around in a circle, and now we're back to where we started. Why was David here? Why did he die?"

"Charlie, maybe he just came here for a vacation."

"It's possible."

"What can I help you with, Charlie? I want to feel useful."

"It might be a good idea to find out more about our 'friend' Malkin. Maybe there was some association between him and David. See what you can find out about him from Deputy O'Rourke."

"Okay, I'll be back in a couple of hours. I may also take a walk on the beach before dinner. Let's have a drink together on the beach and watch the sunset."

"It's a date. I'll meet you at the bar downstairs."

Beth left the room with a smile on her face.

Chapter 12

Suicide?

BEFORE SHE WENT to Police Headquarters, Beth stopped at the hotel David had stayed in. She thought that the manager of the hotel might have some information that would help. When Beth walked toward the front desk, Mr. Parker said, "I'm sorry, Miss, but we don't have any rooms."

"I wasn't looking for a room, but I would like to talk to you about Charlie Anderson, the man who died in your hotel three days ago."

"Are you with the police?" he asked.

"No, I'm his wife."

"Oh, I'm terribly sorry, Ma'am. I'm really sorry about your husband's death."

"Thank you. I wonder if you got to speak to him much. I would like to know what his last days were like. We were separated, and I hadn't spoken to him for awhile. I'm sure the police have already questioned you, but if there's anything important that you remember, please tell me."

"Well, you know, it's strange. The police never came by to ask me any questions."

"They didn't?"

"No. I was surprised. Usually, if there's a death, the police ask about records of phone calls or visitors."

"Do you have records of his phone calls?"

"Sure, but I don't know if I can show them to you."

"I'm a lawyer, Mr. Parker. You don't have to worry about doing something that isn't legal. Charlie is dead, and I am his wife, so you're not breaking the law. You can understand how I feel. I just want to know why he committed suicide."

"I wonder about that myself. He seemed like a happy man," said Parker. "He always said hello and asked about my grandchildren. He talked about the writing he was doing. He said he enjoyed being near the ocean and that it was a wonderful environment for writing."

"Did he tell you what he was writing about?"

"No, but he said it wasn't easy to write about his life. He sure didn't seem sad. In fact, that morning he was supposed to go out on a whale watching boat. The captain of the boat called here and said he never showed up. He tried calling your husband's room and his cell phone, but there was no answer. That's why I went to his room. I thought maybe he had slept late."

"Mr. Parker, did my husband have any visitors?"

"I didn't see anyone, but it's possible. People can go to the rooms without coming through the office.

This is a quiet place, and we've never had any problems."

"Could you show me the record of his calls? As I said before, you're not breaking any laws. I promise you."

"I guess it's all right since you're his wife. I'm sorry. It must be hard for you." He handed her a page showing all the calls made to the room.

"Yes, it's all been a shock. Thank you, Mr. Parker. Here's my card. Call me if you remember anything else."

"Excuse me for asking, Mrs. Anderson, but you don't think he committed suicide, do you?"

"No, I don't."

"You take care of yourself, Mrs. Anderson."

Chapter 13

Sunset on the Beach

CHARLIE WALKED TO THE HOTEL BAR that faced the beach. Beth was already there and watching the sunset. He touched the back of her head. Beth turned and held Charlie's hand.

"Isn't it beautiful, Charlie? Whenever I watch the sunset and see the sky turn orange and pink, I feel the beauty of this world. Then everything bad disappears, and everything good seems possible. I know it's silly, but it's what I think about."

"You never told me that, Beth."

"I never told anyone. Let's drink to the future."

"I'll drink to that. Here's to love, good health, and the time to enjoy them."

"That's nice. Where did you hear that?"

"I learned a Spanish version when I was in South America last year."

"I like it."

"Did you find out anything new about our friend, Malkin?"

"Deputy O'Rourke and I had a nice talk," she said.

"I told him I was sorry about the way I acted this morning. I explained about how stressed I was. I told him I felt responsible for your death because we were separated. He was really sweet. He said that maybe I should get some medicine to calm me down and help me get through this difficult time. We talked about Chief Malkin. The deputy seems to like him, but I think he's getting tired of all the extra hours he's been working lately because Malkin is away from the office a lot."

"Did O'Rourke ever meet David?"

"Yes, as a matter of fact, he did. David apparently wanted to go out on a whaling boat and called Police Headquarters to see if they could recommend one."

"That's strange. Why would he call Police Head-quarters?"

"O'Rourke said David was calling to speak to Malkin. He said he had met him the night before in Nelson's Pub."

"So, Malkin and David knew each other."

"I also spoke to the manager of the hotel David stayed at. He was surprised that the police never came back to question him about phone calls and vis-itors. He's a nice man and didn't think David killed himself. He even gave me a record of all the phone calls that went through the front desk."

"You're amazing, Beth. People really open up to you. The more I learn about Malkin, the less I like him. Something about him troubles me. He's got a story."

"Let's see what facts we know about Malkin," said

Beth. "He's an ex-Marine. He wants to be the mayor of Montauk and thinks like a politician. He met your brother in a bar but acted as if David were a stranger to him. He arrived at David's hotel by himself, so he could have killed David and pretended he was coming from somewhere else. He has no plan to do any further work on this case. He considers it a suicide, which works out nicely for him if he did murder David. Okay, all we need is a motive, a reason for him to kill David."

"Maybe we're looking at this the wrong way, Beth. Let's see what we know about David. He worked for the CIA, he had an accident and was forced to stop working. He came to Montauk either as a spy or to relax and write. He either killed himself or was murdered."

"So we've gone around in a circle again, and we're back to where we started."

"Not quite, Beth. What if Malkin did kill David? We may not know the reason, but we could catch him anyway."

"How do we do that?" Beth asked.

"We trick him. We tell him we know he killed David and that we are going to call the State Police."

"Are you crazy? He'll kill both of us."

"Not if we're careful. This is what I want you to do."

Beth agreed to do what Charlie wanted, and acted as if she was not worried about him. The truth was that she thought his life was in serious danger.

Chapter 14

Setting the Trap

Later that evening, Charlie called Chief Malkin. "Chief, this is Andrew Anderson, Charlie's cousin. I think we need to have a talk. I found some computer files that I think will help you catch the murderer."

"Murderer? Mr. Anderson, your cousin committed suicide. You can read the medical report if you don't believe me."

"Chief Malkin, you didn't know my cousin. I know that someone had a good reason to kill him. I think you'll be interested in seeing these files."

"Okay, Anderson. I'll be over in about fifteen minutes. Are you alone?"

"Yes, why do you ask?"

"I thought his wife might be there, too."

"No, Beth doesn't know about this."

"I'll see you soon, Anderson."

A short while later there was a knock on the door. "Open up, Anderson. It's Chief Malkin."

Charlie opened the door and let Malkin into the room. "Hello, Chief. Would you like a drink?"

"No. I'm here on business. Where are those files?"

"Before I show them to you, I have some questions."

"Are you trying to be the detective here?"

"I need to have some information from you before I give you the files."

"Okay, but hurry up. I don't have all night."

"Did you know my cousin?" asked Charlie.

"No, I never met him before."

"That's strange. Your deputy told us you both met in a bar the night before he died."

"Oh, yeah. I forgot about that."

"Did you know he was on pain medicine?"

"Yeah, he said something about that."

"So you knew he wasn't supposed to drink."

"Listen, what is this all about? Do you have something to show me or are you playing games?"

"I think you killed my cousin. You came to his hotel room and forced him to drink and made it look like a suicide."

"Now why would I do that? I hardly knew the guy."

"He knew something about your past that would hurt your chance of becoming mayor."

"What did you find in his computer? I've been a good cop. I worked hard for years, and now I have a good chance to become mayor. Your cousin didn't stop me and neither will you." Chief Malkin pulled out his gun and pointed it at Charlie.

"What are you going to do, shoot me?" asked Charlie. "How are you going to make this look like a suicide?"

"I'll say you tried to get my gun, and it went off by mistake."

"It won't look good in the newspapers."

"Let me worry about that, Anderson."

"Oh, I'm not worried. It's all here in the computer."

"Not if the computer falls into the pool. Whatever Charlie Anderson wrote can be destroyed. I should have done that before."

"It's too late now, Malkin. I sent copies of his story to the *Boston Globe, New York Times,* and *Montauk News.*"

"What?"

"You're finished, Malkin."

In the distance there was the sound of police sirens. Then there was a knock on the door. Malkin raised the gun. Beth, who was outside the door with the deputy, screamed as she heard the shot. Deputy O'Rourke knocked down the door. Inside the room, Charlie was looking down at Malkin lying on the floor. Malkin's leg was bleeding from a gunshot wound.

"He tried to kill me," Malkin shouted. "He's crazy."

O'Rourke ran over to Chief Malkin. "What happened?"

Charlie was holding the gun. "I tried to grab the gun from him, and it went off. He was trying to shoot me because I accused him of murdering my brother."

O'Rourke looked at Charlie, "I thought he was your cousin."

More sirens could be heard in the distance. Beth ran over to Charlie and held him. She felt him shaking. "Charlie, I thought he shot you. I thought I was losing you all over again."

O'Rourke grabbed the gun from Charlie and was about to hand it to Malkin. Beth stopped him and said, "Deputy, before you hand the gun to your chief, you should hear the whole story. Charlie, tell them who you really are."

"I'm the real Charlie Anderson. The man who supposedly killed himself was my twin brother. We were brought up separately. I didn't even know he existed until I saw his picture in the newspaper. Your chief thought my brother was me, and he killed him so that a scandal of a few years ago stayed hidden. He didn't want to take any chances on ruining his future career as a mayor."

Malkin tried to get up but fell over in pain. "You're the reporter who came here years ago. You're the one I should have killed."

O'Rourke said to Charlie, "You mean he killed the other guy and made it look like a suicide?"

"Be quiet, O'Rourke," ordered Malkin. "Stay out of this."

"That's exactly what I mean. Tell us what happened, Malkin."

"You can talk to my lawyer. I'm not saying anything. Meanwhile, get me to a hospital. Can't you see that I'm wounded?"

"You'll be fine, Malkin. You'll be in great shape to stand trial for my brother's murder."

Chapter 15

Back in Boston

Two days later Beth and Charlie were back in Boston in their old house. They had decided to be together again and work on their marriage. The experience in Montauk made them both realize how much they meant to each other.

"Charlie, you said you'd explain everything to me when we got back to Boston. Why did Chief Malkin kill David?" Beth asked.

"Do you remember when I covered that story about the boys who drowned near Montauk? Malkin was the Chief of Police. I asked a lot of questions about drugs because I thought the boys might have been involved in transporting drugs from yachts that anchored out at sea. I could never prove anything, but I was suspicious. Malkin didn't make it easy for me. I had a feeling he was involved with the drug-running himself."

"But what did that have to do with David?"

"Nothing, except for the fact that he thought David was me. Malkin killed him because he thought he was killing me. He was afraid I would bring up all that past history and ruin his chances of becoming mayor."

"Oh, Charlie, I'm so sorry."

"So am I. I'm sorry my brother had to die before I ever knew him. I'm sorry Malkin thought David was me. David would still be alive today."

"You know, Charlie, maybe you could continue writing the story he started. It would be a tribute to his memory, and you'll get to know him even better."

"I think there may be a reason that fate brought us together again. Maybe I will write about David's life. It's the least I can do for my brother. Maybe this will be the book I was supposed to write."

Chapter 16

What Really Happened

It was July 7. Police Chief Malkin was sitting in a bar having a beer. It was Sunday, and he was off duty. David Anderson walked into the bar and sat next to the chief. They said hello and continued drinking. David was very friendly and asked the chief if he was visiting Montauk, too.

"No, I've lived here all my life," said Malkin. "Where are you from? What brings you to Montauk?"

"I'm from the Midwest, but I've lived all over. I always wanted to see the beaches here and do a little fishing. I also want to go whale watching."

"What kind of work do you do?" asked Malkin.

"Oh, I do a little of this and a little of that."

"You're a man with secrets."

"Let's say I've been around. I was in the military, and then I worked for the government."

"And now what do you do?"

"Now I'm on permanent disability. I was in a car accident and broke some bones in my back. I haven't worked in a year."

"Lucky you," laughed Malkin.

"I wasn't so lucky. I still have a lot of pain, and I take pretty strong pain pills."

"Are you supposed to drink?

"Not really, but once in a while I cheat. So far, I haven't gotten into trouble. I don't drink very much."

"Are you sure we never met before? You look very familiar."

"I've never been here before. Maybe I have a familiar face."

"Yeah, maybe that's it. What's your name?"

"David Gilden. What's yours?"

"Paul Malkin."

"So, what do you do?"

"I'm a cop.

"Really, I bet you have some interesting stories."

"Not too many. This is a pretty quiet town most of the year."

"No criminals for you to arrest?

"We have occasional drunk drivers and some teenagers who get a little wild."

"No murders."

"Not since I've been here."

"Well, let's hope it stays quiet while I'm here on vacation."

"I'll do my best. Anyway, see you around." Chief Malkin finished his drink and got up to leave. "By the way, where are you staying?"

"I'm at the Beachcomber. It's pretty basic, but the view is great."

"Well, enjoy yourself. I'll see you around."

Chief Malkin headed for his car and thought about David Gilden.

"I know that guy. I don't know why he's pretending he doesn't know me. He doesn't fool me one bit. He's playing it cool, but I know he's up to something. He probably knows I'm running for mayor. I wonder if someone hired him to check up on me. He's probably going to dig up something about those three boys who drowned about five years ago. Yeah, that's why I remember him. His name isn't Gilden. It's Anderson. He's that reporter who came down from New York City. I remember him snooping around and asking a lot of questions. He thought the boys may have been using drugs. Little did he know they were running drugs for me.

"But I've been away from that stuff for years. I'm a respectable Chief of Police, and soon I'll be mayor. No newspaper reporter is going to destroy this for me. I've worked hard, and I have earned this. The election is only a few months away. I'm not going to let this guy Anderson kill my chances. He said he was staying at the Beachcomber. I think we're going to have another drink together very soon."